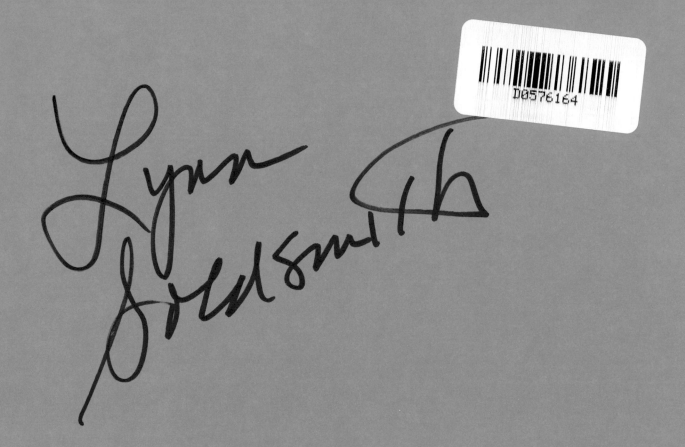

First published in the United States of America in 1991
by RIZZOLI INTERNATIONAL PUBLICATIONS, INC.
300 Park Avenue South, New York, NY 10010

Copyright © 1991 by Lynn Goldsmith

ISBN: 0-8478-1447-5

Designed by Elizabeth Van Itallie

Printed and bound by Dai Nippon, Tokyo, Japan

May all your days be circus days.

CIRCUS

BY LYNN

CIRCUS SOUVENIRS & GIFTS

FOR CHILDREN

The circus fascinates millions of people because it touches the imagination, the spirit, the soul. It is magic. For centuries, circuses have enchanted everyone, but no circus event has captivated quite so many hearts as the Great Circus Parade. This week-long celebration of circus the way it used to be is the grandest event of its kind. It brings back to life an almost forgotten chapter of our heritage.

Every July, a half-mile of Americana takes to the tracks when seventy-five priceless antique circus wagons are loaded by teams of Percheron horses onto a string of vintage flatcars at the Circus World Museum in Baraboo, Wisconsin, original home of the Ringling Brothers. This ceremony takes two days of hard physical labor by the museum staff with the help of volunteer circus fans. The caravan is routed to show off the wagons to over forty communities. It travels for two days via a roundabout 222 mile route through southern Wisconsin and northern Illinois. As it rolls by, the Great Circus Train gives the waiting young and old a real look at circus history.

When the train arrives in Milwaukee, the grand and colorful wagons are unloaded by draft horses in traditional, turn-of-the-century style. They're placed on the showgrounds where for three days prior to the Great Circus Parade, the public can view them, touch them, take pictures of them. Encircled by the wagons is the Midway, which is alive all day long with bandwagons, animal rides, and circus acts. Crowning the festivities are four shows a day under the Big Top of the Royal Hanneford Circus. Aerialists dance in the air, elephants sit upright on stools, ferocious lions obediently jump through hoops of fire, and clowns fly off the

OF ALL AGES...

backs of prancing horses.

On Sunday, the seventh day, the spectacle begins. The Great Circus Parade is probably the largest animated historic museum display ever conceived and carried off. Just about all of these wagons have paraded down main streets of America in the past century. It can be likened to Flo Ziegfeld going to the old ladies' home where his former famous chorus line resided and saying: "OK girls, on your feet. We're going through the routine once more." To see these magnificent examples of American folk art actually moving through the street makes people feel they are living in the golden days of the circus. Seven hundred horses and scores of wild animals, circus performers, clowns, and bands join together in a larger-than-life salute to a spectacle that was larger than life to begin with. For two hours the sights, sounds, and smells of a bygone era return. It delivers glory.

There are 2500 volunteers who participate in the Great Circus Parade. It is organized by a non-profit foundation. There are no product commercials allowed. Several hundred individuals and corporations agree not to display so much as a logo and collaborate to pay the bill for this most American of parades. In a time when our society seems to be motivated to give only with the idea of what can be gotten in return, the Great Circus Parade is an example of people working together for a common good, working together without egos, working together because of a mutual love. America was built by people who had dreams of what life could be at its best. Neighbors helped each other to make those dreams a reality. The circus still breathes through the Great Circus Parade, and so does the spirit of America. – Lynn Goldsmith

THE

TRAIN

The long, low note of the train's horn sounds in the distance.

Baraboo precisely on schedule, actually a minute ahead of time, at 9:14 a.m.

THE train – half a mile and 26 flatcars long – left

People wait at every railroad crossing as though welcoming an old friend.

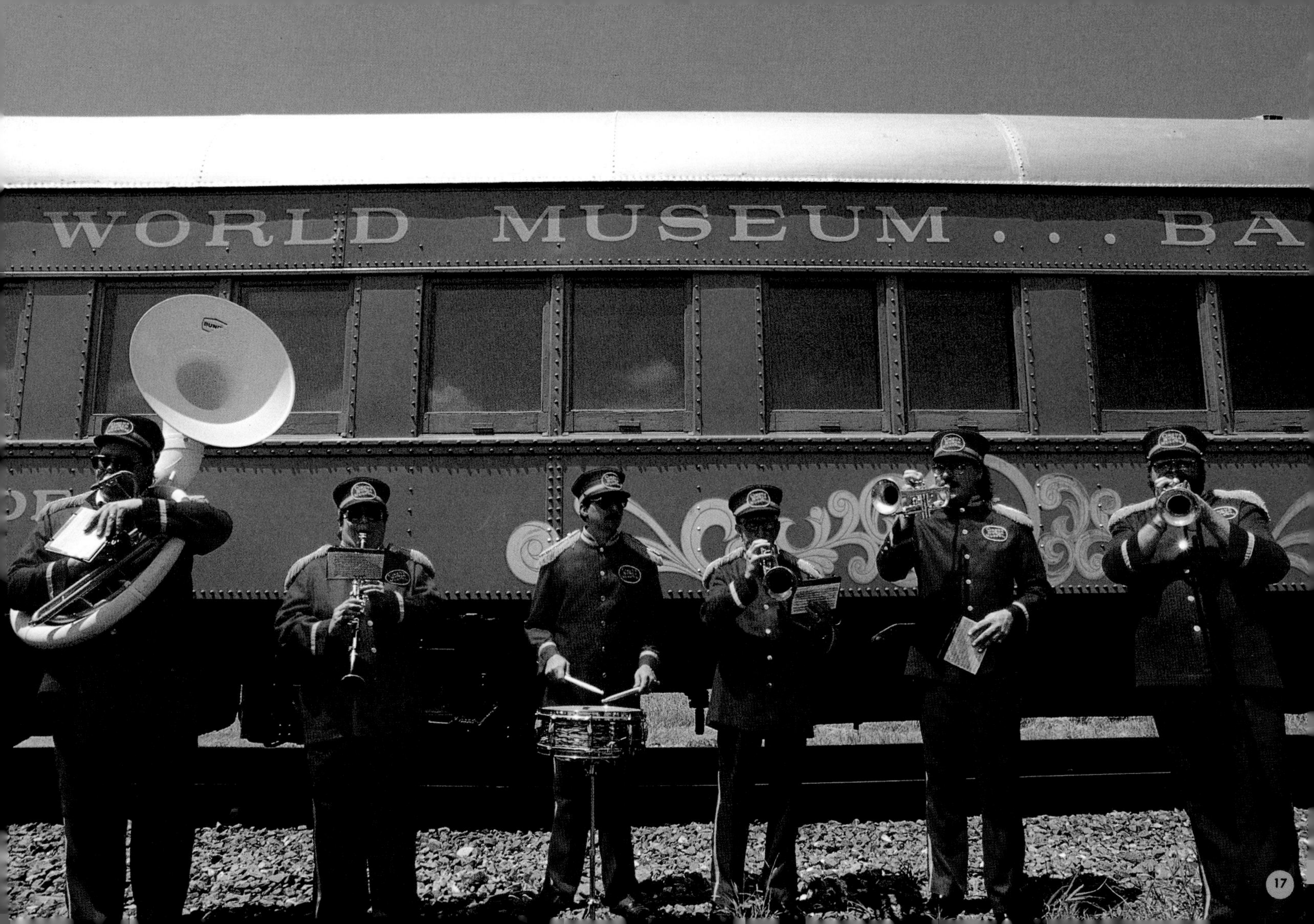
WORLD MUSEUM . . . BA

There are mothers with babes in arms, fathers with tykes sitting on their shoulders, families sprawled out on blankets…

It's magic. We put all of the pennies we've collected on to the tracks, so when the great circus train rolls over 'em, they become like little potato chips.

AFTER THE SLOW-MOVING TRAIN PARADED PAST, JUSTIN LEANED BACK AGAINST HIS MOTHER AND SIGHED. 'THAT MADE ME DIZZY,' HE ANNOUNCED.

...A MIGHTY

millionaire eye-feast; in splendor 'rich beyond the dreams of avarice.' A winding, dazzling river of silver and gold. An immense cavalcade of red-plumed horses burdened with costly trappings and caravan of princely wealth on heavy rumbling wheels. New chariots, gorgeous with gilded lion and serpent, or carved with dolphins and dragons, and griffins and hippo-griffins. New tableau cars, four squared with Grecian gods and goddesses, or illuminated with golden sea-horses, winged leopards, mermaids, and fabulous figures. New animal wagons, ornate with designs from the dreams of Hesiod, and carvings grotesque, arabesque, and picturesque. Classical figures of triple graces playing harps and trumpets, and raised designs of silver horses necked with golden manes. Triumphal floats and barges with medallioned mythical faces...Peruvian sun gods, centaurs, moon-men, golden calves, and Chinese dragon day glories. – Ringling Bros. route book, 1892

CHILE · ARGENTINA · BRAZIL · RINGLING BROS. · WESTERN HEMISPHERE · MEXICO · CANADA · UNITED STATES

35

A FELLOW

from Chicago came into the shop one day and asked if we could build some circus wagons for him. I allowed we could and told him all we needed to know was the length, height, style, and load they were to carry. With that the fellow proceeded to unroll a mess of blueprints he had under his arm. He told me we would have to follow these plans to the letter. So I told him to take his damn plans and go back to Chicago. What I didn't tell him was that I couldn't read the blueprints if I tried. – Henry Moeller, Jr., wagon builder

The wagons require constant  them and damage the paint.

care and repainting every three years

Hot and humid weather can warp

or so. That doesn't mean a touch-up job either. It means repainting the whole thing.

HECK,

I go back to before they even had a Circus World Museum. Like everybody else there, I was a circus fan from childhood, and when I was given a chance to work on the parade crew, I jumped at it. I worked all of the Milwaukee parades in the '60s and early '70s, as well as the Chicago ones, and I thought it was terrific when they started it up again in 1985. I can't think of a better three-week vacation than this.

I CHECK

in July 5 and work through July 21 at one thing or another, in addition to loading and unloading the train. My wife, Rosalind, joins in, working in the cookhouse tent on the show grounds in Milwaukee. And my daughter Kay comes in from Tacoma, Wash., where her husband is in the army at Fort Lewis, also to work in the cookhouse. So it's an annual get-together for us, built around the parade. It's great seeing all the other circus buffs, and having your own family involved makes it even better.

You know the image of a kid wistfully looking at a circus tent from the

outside, wishing he could get in? Well, I feel I'm the lucky kid who got in.

THE C

IRCUS

The Midway is where the action is...
band organ concerts, food stands, petting zoo,
elephant and camel rides, horse tents,
and the 'cannonball thrill' act.

THERE

was a big thunderstorm the night before. I think my mother was more nervous than we were. There were two 35-ton cranes fully extended, 90 to 100 feet above the ground. It was our first double skywalk, and Debbie's first skywalk ever. Afterwards we felt ecstatic. We'd done something no one had ever done before. One of the volunteers, Bill Rotzoll, who is president of our fan club, held one of the ropes and almost had cardiac arrest.

get to know you. They're not afraid, but they're leery at first. But after they do get to

Not just any stranger can walk up to them. They have to

know you they'll try to stick your hand in their mouths.

People say llamas spit all the time. But usually, all they're doing is clearing their nasal passages. They grow on you.

HUNDREDS of sweating horses;

strange scents from animals from all over the world seeping from cages and dens,

the unusual essence that wafts to the nostrils as 40 elephants shuffle by.

And the smell of 15 or 20 camels can't be described. – Charles Philip Fox

I told my Mom I wasn't gonna wash it off for a week, but she said, 'What about the pillowcase?'

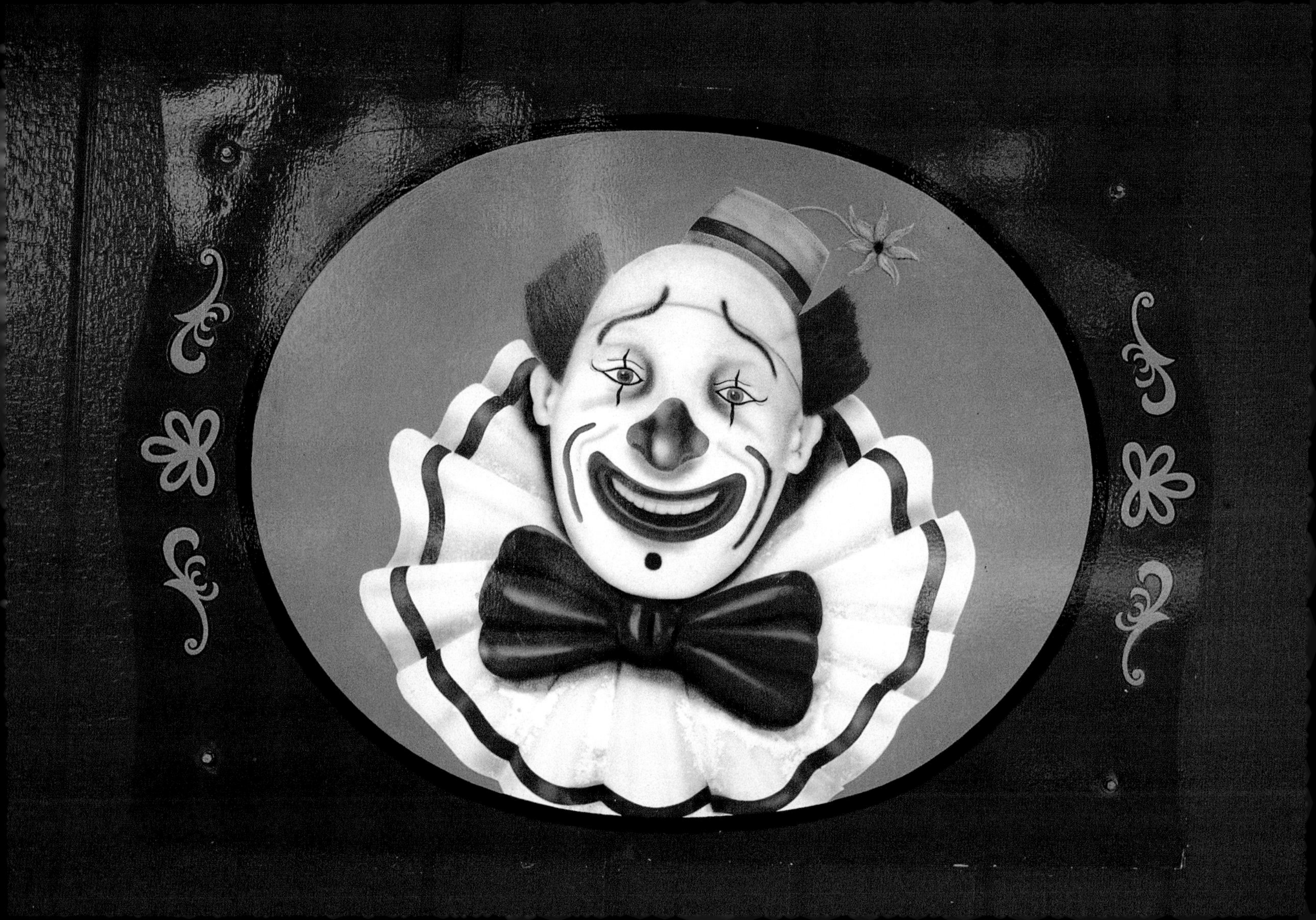

All I wanted
to do was to make
people laugh.
My life's
calling was to
be a clown.

THERE

are two things I love – my daughter Chelsea and the circus. I started off as a clown and then kept looking at the ringmaster thinking, 'Why can't a woman do that?' I asked if they would give me a try. I said, 'If I'm lousy, give me gas money, but if I'm good please give me a contract.' The first date I worked was 10 years ago in Boston, Mass., and out of it came a two-year contract *and* gas money.

My family is the longest-running dynasty in circus history, and we are the last. It is going on 300 years that the Royal Hanneford Circus has performed across the globe.

SAWDUST, SPANGLES AND DREAMS, POPCORN AND CRACKERJACKS PLAY A PART. EVERYTHING GLEAMS UNDER THE BIG TOP THAT'S IN YOUR HEART.

Charles Philip Fox, or "Chappie" as he is affectionately called, is considered to be the number one authority on circus life. He, on the other hand, considers himself to be a lifetime student of the circus. He has authored many books on the circus and is the founder of the Circus World Museum. Chappie believes that seeing, smelling, and experiencing a circus assures

people of all ages that life holds possibilities other than the ones they already know. The Great Circus Parade is a manifestation of his vision and persistence. No one dreamed that such a spectacular re-creation of the historical circus street procession could ever happen, 'til C.P. Fox made his dream come true. Keep on dreaming circus dreams Chappie...we love you.

THE P

ARADE

Showcasing the horsemanship that has long been the centerpiece of the circus, the Two Hemispheres wagon is pulled by forty Belgian horses. That's 720 feet of leather and two fistfuls of reins.

Managing a team of 40
horses is a challenge. Each
horse has a personality of its
own and an attitude about
pleasing. Many young
horses work well alone
but must be taught to
conform to the regimen-
tation of the line.

IT'S A COMBINATION

of manpower and horsepower. Each horse weighs about a ton. To pull the wagons, we needed giant Clydesdales, Percherons, and Belgians, trained to work in teams. They said we'd never find them and if we did, how could we afford to bring them all to Wisconsin? Horse people rallied and word of mouth drew volunteer teams from 10 states. They just do it out of pride. Nobody else in the world does this.

The horses are washed, curried, and brushed. Their manes and tails are combed and styled.

They enter the wardrobe tents in street clothes and emerge as kings, queens, glittering show people.

Everyone who has purchased a red clown's nose for $1 is reminded to wear it 11 a.m. to 1 p.m.

THIS

is not just another parade. This is our heritage in the form of an heirloom that when dusted and polished belongs to us all.

The girls have the long white gloves. So it's a very definite feminine look. Ladies wear jeans and all, but I'm sorry, I think people still like to see girls in dresses and hats and looking like girls.

There are no barricades at all. Everything is within your grasp which

means one thing...stake out your territory really early for the best view.

They're making bets on where the road apples will fall. Road apples?

You could call them souvenirs that the circus animals are bound to leave!

THE 1963 PARADE WAS GREAT, BUT WE HAD NOTHING TO COMPARE IT WITH. AS EACH YEAR WENT BY WE GOT BETTER, BIGGER, AND MORE ORGANIZED.

We will be soaked
when we are done,
believe me. If
you could feel the
weight of some of
these costumes, you
would fall over.

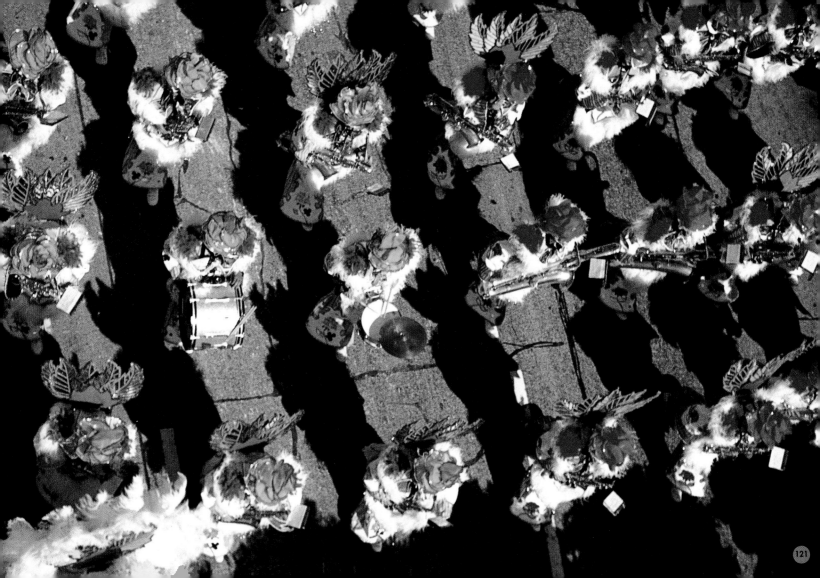

**IF** any vehicle breaks down in parade,

pull to one side and after fixed up, get in anywhere, but do not stop parade

.... Every employee that is not in parade and is not active on the lot, must be stationed along the line of parade

telling people to look out for their horses

.... Drivers watch your teams

.... Drivers must be cleanshaven and have their boots blackened when time permits

.... No smoking or chewing.

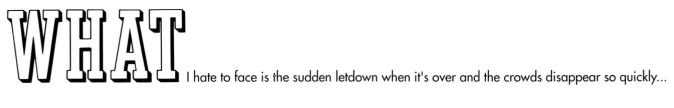

WHAT I hate to face is the sudden letdown when it's over and the crowds disappear so quickly...

CREDIT PAGES

8 Arthur Brothers Circus Den, 1920.

22 Jolly the Clown – Art Petrie.

24 Royal Bengal Tigers Den, 1915.

25 Black Maned Nubian Lions Den, 1905.

26 Twin Lion Telescoping Tableau, 1865.

27 Barnum and Bailey Tableau Den, 1885.

28 Many of the retired Ringling Circus craftsmen living in Baraboo came together to restore the historic wagons.

30 The detail work is some of the finest examples of folk art to date.

32 Old Lady in the Shoe Nursery Float, 1885.

33 Mother Goose Nursery Float, 1885.

34 Elephant Tableau, 1920.

35 Two Hemispheres Bandwagon, 1902.

36 Pawnee Bill Bandwagon, 1903. Gordon Lillie was Pawnee Bill.

37 Asia Tableau, 1903.

38 Detail from Pawnee Bill Tableau – every circus wagon was the same on both sides except for this one. The center carving was of Columbus discovering America and the other side was Pocahantas saving John Smith.

39 The Columbia Bandwagon, 1898.

40 Wagon wheels – called sunburst wheels. V-shaped pieces of wood were painted from the narrow end, starting with red into orange, then into yellow. As the wheel revolved, it looked like the sun's rays.

42 Mechanical bandorgan, 1900. Used on the Midway.

43 St. George and the Dragon, 1865. Replica from woodcarving of Lion and Mirror Wagon.

44 Don and Harold Krueger.

46 Volunteers, many of whom spend their summer vacations working to make the parade happen.

47 Volunteer – Bill McFann.

50 Clown – Keith Crary.

52 Human cannonball – Luis Munoz.

54 High wire artists – Enrico and Debbie Wallenda.

56 Elephant trainer – Peter Mortensen.

57 Elephant trainer – Karen Cristiani.

58 Oxen owner – Charles Robb.

66 Children's face painter – Reyna Flores.

70 Painting and flags from Baraboo Circus World Museum.

72 Clown – Russell Brown.

74 Ringmaster – Charlie and daughter Chelsea Hackett.

75 Tommy Hanneford.

76 Trapeze artists – Lorraine and Martha Flores.

77 Elizabeth Rodrigues.

78 Equestriennes – Kathy Hayes and Carla Zoppe.

79 Evy Karoly – teacher, mother, friend to all.

81 Mark Karoli and wife.

83 Lion tamer – Jorge Barreda.

84 Contortionist – Hugo Zamarotte.

88 Chappie Fox – I took my quote about Flo Ziegfeld in the introduction from him; what better source than the driving force of the Great Circus Parade!

93 The forty-horse hitch driven by Dick and Paul Sparrow.

99 Tail of the Anheuser Busch Clydesdale.

102 Volunteer clowns.

104 Seashell Tableau, 1914. Betsy Ross Tableau, built in 1965 to add to patriotic section.

106 Rainbow Equestriennes.

112 Baraboo High School Marching Band.

113 Woodland String Band.

116 Six man bicycle – the bachelors from Algonia.

117 Star Tableau, 1890.

122 Parade rules from 1904 – Walter L. Main Circus.

123 U.S. Navy Flag Unit.

Horsemanship has long been the centerpiece of the circus. With your help, the Great Circus Parade marches on.

Vernon Albert
Anheuser Busch Co.
Ray Bast
The Lynte & Harry Bradley
    Foundation
Elroy Brass
Merle Brooks
John Carlson
Devere Clay
Robert Clay
Ralph Coddington
Barry Dickenson
Bruce Duchossioss
Robert Ehnerd
Art Eller
John Fairclough
William Farmer
Keeland Farms
Merle Fischer
Roy Fox
Ann Friend
Al Gagliano
Lyle Getschman
Ned Hahn

Holden Hankee
Jay Hankee
William E. Hauser
Lester Johnson
Dan Jones
Richard Koltz
Harold Krueger
Calvin Larson
Wayne Laurensen
Ann Leck
Rich Lee
Robert Litscher
Dale Lockwood
Mary Ruth Marks
Harold Moritz
Pat Morrison
Stanley Piper
Tip Porter
Earl Prochnow
Russell Punge
Sharon Riemer
Roland Ruby
Otis Ruff
Richard Savatski
Bud Schmidt
Dean Schmidt
Harold Schumacher
Ralph Schwartz
Thomas Schwartz
Paul Stitt
Lloyd Stoeklen
Paul Waseelewski
Wisconsin Morgan Horse Club
Wayne Withers
Keith Woodbury

When the nation was younger, the traveling circus was perhaps the only entertainment a community would have all year. Today the circus has nearly all but died out, thus the circus parade was destined to become a memory until Charles Philip Fox realized he was on a mission. He knew he had to fulfill his dream of bringing back, true to its original form, the circus parade. With the devoted help of Ben Barkin and the dedication of volunteers who shared that dream, real history comes to life each year at the Great Circus Parade.

Tova and Ernest Borgnine –
Grand Clowns

THANK YOU ALL

Ben Barkin, founding organizer and trustee. "Anyone who sees how the countryside is lined with people as the circus train moves through Wisconsin and Illinois would feel a tremendous lift in their spirits. Children on the shoulders of grandparents, people in wheelchairs waving, even the blind come to feel the train pass by. It is an unbelievable sight. I am delighted to be able to be a part of the scene."

Charles Philip Fox,
Sophie and Barbara
Ben Barkin
National Geographic Traveler
Milwaukee Sentinel
Milwaukee Journal
Bob and Greg Parkinson
Jack Varick
Joe Weinfurter
H.J. (Jim) Morrill
Joanne K. Peterson
Mike Bartel
Peg Coburn
Struppi and Nellie Hanneford
Bobby Moore
John Zweifel

Kay Rosaire
Nikon Professional
Camera Services
Charles Miers
Bruno Nesci
Choo Choo Kim
Gabriel Perle
The photography in this book was supported, in part, by the Professional Photography Division, Eastman Kodak Co.
Special thanks to Ray DeMoulin and Charles Styles for their trust in me.

Lynn Goldsmith was introduced to the Great Circus Parade through an assignment by National Geographic Traveler. What she saw was an important reminder that dreams can come true. "I saw how people worked in unison to keep the circus alive. I saw families sharing their joy of it. I saw the heart of America. Thanks, Mom for taking me and Ellen to our first circus."